SECRETS
FROM THE GREENROOM

A Comedian's Inside Techniques for Effective Speaking

And now ladies and gentlemen for the first time ever...

SECRETS
From the Greenroom

A Comedian's Inside Techniques
for Effective Speaking

DAVID MICHAEL

WORD ASSOCIATION PUBLISHERS
www.wordassociation.com
1.800.827.7903

Printed in the United States of America.

ISBN: 978-1-59571-733-7
Library of Congress Control Number: 2011938039

Designed and published by

Word Association Publishers
205 Fifth Avenue
Tarentum, Pennsylvania 15084

www.wordassociation.com
1.800.827.7903

To

my mother and father,

my sisters Cassie and Suzanne,

...and to Beth and Ryan

CONTENTS

ACKNOWLEDGMENTS

never planned to write a book. And I certainly couldn't have done it alone. This book would never have seen the light of day without the love and support of my family and a few key people. In addition to my mother, my father, my sisters Cassie and Suzanne, and to Beth and Ryan, I would like to thank Aunt Peg and Uncle Joe, my cousin Pat Gales, and my grandmother Elaine.

I would like to thank Coleen and Steve Baldwin, Sharon and Dale Hess, and a very special thanks to Barb and Bill Peters.

Many thanks also to my talent agent, David Sedelmeier, and all the folks at Talent Network: Frank Murgia, Kathleen Morris, Kelly Reginelli, Linda Venezie, Megan Montanaro, and Emma Venezie.

I am grateful to Word Association Publishers for guiding me through the mysteries of the publishing process, including Tom Costello, Jason Price, and my editor, the fabulous Nan Newell.

I would especially like to thank Vince Mangini, my friend of twenty-five years, for helping me to structure the book. I will be forever indebted to him for his insights, his honesty, his patience, his writing abilities, and his uncanny knack for creating order out of chaos. I couldn't have written the book without him.

And finally, a huge thank-you to all the famous and not-so-famous comedians (see inside cover) I have worked with over the years, for showing me how to leave an audience wanting more.

INTRODUCTION

"Your next performer has worked from coast to coast, appeared on national television, and acted in a few feature films... Please help me welcome from Pittsburgh, Pennsylvania... David Michael!"

Wow. That's me! It's funny when you see it in writing. It's hard to believe how far I've come when I reflect on my professional life—from the times I worked for free, doing open stages in dingy little clubs, to performing in front of thousands of people in concert halls, and along the way, meeting thousands of fans and befriending some of comedy's biggest stars. It has been a wild ride and one that I continue to this day.

You are actually holding my next goal in your hands—that's to be an author. I'm not an author yet, but I will be by the time you finish this book. I have to confess, I never thought I'd be an author. But there was something inside me stirring that I had to get out. The concept for this book has been rattling around in my head for years, and I'm surprised that no one thought of it before. I believe I can help you become a better public speaker by showing you how comedic techniques can be used to get your message across. I don't intend to do this simply by telling you some good jokes that have worked well with an audience, but rather by letting you in on tricks of the trade that I have learned along the way—both from my own experience as a comedian and from some of the biggest names in comedy.

So what qualifies me to write this book? I would say that it's all that I learned from performing at thousands of corporate gigs, sales presentations, business fairs, and expos. And all that I learned from listening to motivational speakers who were trying in vain to connect with their audience. It was shocking to see how unimaginative, boring, and lackluster most of these people were. As an entertainer, I could relate to their plight. I'd been there myself a thousand times before. I know what it's like to have the challenge of connecting with an audience, figuring how to make them laugh, and ultimately getting the message across. So I am the first to sympathize with the guy at the podium.

Bad performances by young comedians are nothing compared to the sales seminars that I had to endure. I spent mindnumbing afternoons listening to speakers drone on and on about how they could make me—and you can fill in the blank—more efficient, more motivated, a better salesman, a better team player, etc. All of the time I kept thinking, "These people are getting big bucks and they have no idea how to connect with the audience." I kept asking myself, "Why doesn't he engage the audience?" or "Why doesn't he use a call-back?"— simple techniques that comedians use all the time. (A call-back is a joke that refers to a previously told joke. Many times a joke will get a bigger laugh the second time around.) Then it hit me, these guys don't know the tricks of the trade. They don't know how to reel in an audience. They don't know the techniques that comedians and entertainers use all the time to bridge the gap between the stage and the crowd.

Public speakers and comedians alike need the audience to listen to us and come away with a message. The only difference is that we comedians need a *physical* response from the audience. We need them to laugh. And that's what makes it easy to gauge how a comedian is doing. You walk into a comedy club and you either hear the laughter or you don't. It's not so easy when someone is addressing a business crowd. I want to help turn your presentation into something that the crowd will respond to and remember.

The same tactics and strategies that I use as a comedian can be utilized in all interactions, from a a college student making a class presentation to a salesman looking to close a deal. Even if public speaking is not part of your normal job routine, you may be called upon to address a crowd in your social life. Perhaps you have to make the toast at a 25th wedding anniversary. Who knows? If you have to communicate with people in any situation, I can help.

OK. Relax. This book is *not*—I repeat—this book is *not* going to make you a comedian. It may make you a little funnier and it certainly will increase your ability to gauge an audience. My goal is to make you a more effective, more entertaining speaker. It pains me to see a bright, successful person giving a lackluster presentation. Being able to speak in front of a group of people is the single most important attribute you can have in business. If you can speak well in front of a group, and actually communicate with them (because that's what it's all about—communication), you will be more effective, more successful than everyone around you and I guarantee that.

I'm going to share with you the tricks and techniques comedians use every day and night and show you how you can incorporate them into your presentation, your speech, your toast—any situation where you have to talk in front of a crowd. What I will reveal will help you in every facet of your life. You'll come away with more self-confidence. Your creative juices will begin to flow. You will begin to take chances and not worry about failing.

I'm also going to show you how your audience has been conditioned to learn. Don't worry, I'm not going to delve into any psychological theory. That's not my expertise. I'm not a scientist or a researcher by any means. I don't have any statistics nor have I ever conducted any experiments. All I can offer is real world experience. I've performed countless shows and have been on stage thousands of times. I know what works. These are tried and true secrets that entertainers use to grab an audience's attention, hold it, and make them remember their message.

If your ultimate goal is to communicate with your audience (or if you are a salesman, to get your audience to buy your product), you have to have a basic understanding of how an audience receives and retains your message. Once you grasp this, your speaking job will become a whole lot easier.

I'm also going to show you how to stimulate your innate creativity, how to get you to think outside the box. If I can get you as a speaker to be a little more entertaining than the rest of the speakers out there, you will be well on your way.

When you read this book I want you to try to keep in mind at all times that when you are speaking you're not just delivering a speech or presentation you're giving a performance. So these secrets I offer are powerful ways of connecting with your audience. Also keep in mind the ways in which you can use these techniques to enhance your performance. Remember it's the audience that's important and your entertaining them will keep them focused on what you have to say. So remember: performance, creativity, and audience.

My big goal here is to make you an effective communicator. One of the keys to achieving this goal is brevity. So let's get movin'. I hope you enjoy the ride.

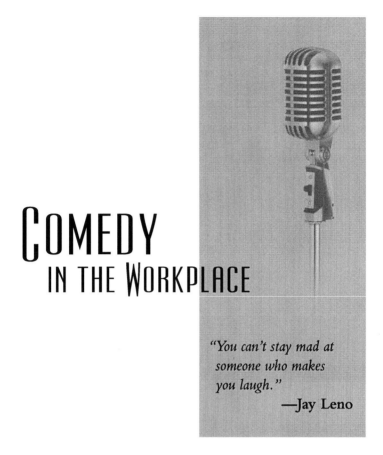

COMEDY
IN THE WORKPLACE

*"You can't stay mad at
someone who makes
you laugh."*
—Jay Leno

People may ask the question, are comedians relevant in the business world? I would say that the services and expertise that we can provide make us uniquely qualified to help businesses. Over the last twenty years comedians have become more relied upon as experts in the workplace and not just as entertainers.

My first foray into the business world was a unique challenge. Early in my comedy career a friend approached me after a show and asked if I could do my comedy act in a business setting. I immediately thought it would not be a problem. How hard could it be to make a few suits laugh? The guy who asked me was an out-of-the-box-type thinker.

He was a manager at a major manufacturing company. He was twenty-eight at the time and the next closest manager to him in age was over fifty years old. He rose to his position because he was smart and he wasn't afraid to take risks—such as bringing in a stand-up comic instead of one more motivational speaker!

After I agreed to do the show, I found out that I would be performing for the workers, not the management. And I would do my comedy set in the middle of a work shift. These weren't ideal conditions for comedy, but I would be getting a nice check. I did the show during the workers' lunch break. The show went over really well. It went over so well that my friend decided to make the comedy show a monthly event.

After six months my friend reviewed his production reports and employee satisfaction surveys. The data revealed that he had almost no call-offs on the day of the show as well as below-normal absenteeism on the days before and after the show. Productivity increased along with employee job satisfaction. At the time I didn't realize how much effect a little humor could have on a work force. Thinking back, I guess my resourceful friend had come up with his own take on an employee wellness program. The experience opened my eyes to how comedy can make for a better workplace environment and improve employee performance and satisfaction.

A few years later one of my corporate clients asked a special favor. This company was merging with another large company and the executives wanted me to entertain at a social where the employees of the two organizations would meet for the first time. This was going to be a challenge because everyone in the room knew that their lives were about to change. Some of the people in the room would not be retained, some of them would have their job descriptions revamped, and some would be asked to relocate to a different city. The CEOs from both companies were very nervous and did not know what to expect from their employees. They told me my job was to ease the tension in the room and make the people feel good about what was going on. Thanks, guys. So what could I do to cut stress in the room? I decided to make fun of the executives who made the decision to merge. I figured having two people mad at me was better than two entire companies.

At most corporate gigs the organizers sit near the front, off to a side. Everyone in the crowd can see them. And if the bigwigs don't laugh, the rest of the crowd won't laugh either.

I opened up with material that I knew would get a mild response. The executives didn't laugh at all. I stopped the show and said, "These guys up front are responsible for the merger. They hired me to reduce the stress and they're sitting there stone-faced. They remind me of two guys I used to see on the road all the time." I then flashed a photo behind me of the two old guys from The Muppet Show who sat in the balcony. The crowd went nuts. This little joke acted as a release. The rest of the show went great.

I still get a good feeling from what I was able to do that night. I think my humor helped to defuse a volatile situation.

Comedians are also in demand in the world of advertising. I have a dear friend who moonlighted as a comedian while holding down a job at an advertising firm. Over the years, his "regular" job won out, but he keeps me abreast of industry articles on comedy in advertising and humorous ad campaigns. Advertising executives often use comedians in their ad campaigns and they hire comedians to write funny material for their ads. Think back to your favorite commercials—I bet they were funny.

The old saying that laughter is the best medicine rings true. There have been numerous clinical studies that show how laughing can improve a person's health. Most people can cite Norman Cousins's book or the movie based on the story of real-life Doctor Patch Adams. Doctors are now administering therapeutic humor as a way to give patients relief from stress and pain and improve their sense of well-being. I know of a physician who prescribed four comedy movies for a patient as an antidote for stress. The results were so impressive that to this day this person makes a point to have some type of humor in his life every day.

There has to be room for comedy or humor in the workplace. It doesn't have to be a fifteen-minute performance by a comedian. It could be as simple as a joke of the day or a wacky shirt contest. Every place of employment needs to have something that helps to relieve job-related stress. It's comforting to me that my profession has grown from strictly entertaining people to improving their health.

Comedians have also evolved into experts in the world of verbal communications. It is widely accepted that comedians work at the highest level of speaking. More and more in the past few years we have been relied upon to help executives and the general public write, punch up and create presentations as well as delivering keynote speeches ourselves. All of which, has culminated in the writing of this book!

GETTING STARTED

"Never be afraid to try something new. Remember, amateurs built the ark. Professionals built the Titanic."

—Drew Carey

F irst of all, you should be speaking about (or selling) something that interests you and that you believe in. It's hard to convince an audience to come to your side unless you are truly committed to what you are talking about. You have to be able to stand in front of the crowd and speak from your heart. I don't mean you have to be gushy, because if you are, you risk coming off as a phony. Be honest and sincere. One of the best ways to develop a quick bond with an audience is to give examples of your faults. It's been said that we learn more from our mistakes than from the things we do right. Let the audience know what you have done wrong and how you corrected it and what you learned. Doing that makes you more credible.

You have to figure out what your purpose is. Are you trying to prompt them to action, sway their opinion, disseminate information, or simply entertain them?

You also have to consider the expectations of the audience. Why are they attending? Are they there because their boss forced them to come? Are they paying out of their own pockets or is the company picking up the tab? Are they mandated to be there because of a court order? (I'll say more about this audience later in the book.)

The speech needs to have a structure: a beginning, a middle, and an end. The opening should have some kind of attention-grabbing statement or story and close with a call to action or a memorable message. That message should be clear and concise. You want to use concrete examples to bring life to the points you want to make. And you don't have to limit yourself to the spoken word. There's nothing wrong with a few visual aids to help get your point across.

Don't be afraid to be different. Imagine how tiresome the comedy world would be if every comedian sounded alike or had the same delivery. There'd be no place for Emo Philips, Steven Wright, Bobcat Goldthwait, or even the sly intonations of Johnny Carson. In the current world of public speaking, there may be different speakers, but they all sound the same. Now, you don't want to go overboard and be the weird guy, or have your message lost because the crowd only remembers your shtick. But you do want to engage the audience. Don't be afraid to move about the stage. Don't be afraid to be creative.

Practice your speech so that the words flow easily from memory. Occasionally glancing down at your note cards is okay, but you definitely **do not** want to read your speech. A good way to memorize your presentation is to write it out. This helps to imprint the words on your brain. You should videotape or, at the very least, tape record your practice sessions and review them. Take note of how fast you talk, how many ums or mumbles there are. The video is a good way to review your facial expression and body posture and to correct unnecessary hand gestures. You want to be certain that you know your lines and that your volume, pace, and tone are appropriate.

People often ask me, "How do you remember all that stuff?" Every performer has a different way to remember their material. I developed a technique that I call "blocking." I try to write jokes around a particular subject—for example, dating. As I write more and more jokes on the subject, I try to have them flow seamlessly together. When I have five to seven minutes of material on the subject I have a block. So for a 40-minute show I need six or seven blocks of material. All I have to do is remember the five or seven minutes in each block. I memorize one block at a time. That way, I'm breaking down a lot of material into manageable pieces that I can move around within a show.

I use two methods to remember the jokes or stories that make up the blocks. I usually write out the piece first. I then practice telling the joke to myself over and over again. Along the way I might change some words or my voice inflection, perfecting the joke. Once I'm comfortable with the material I write it out again. (I also type my jokes onto my computer, but that's just for record keeping.) There's something about writing it out in longhand that helps to hardwire the information into your brain.

Another memory technique that works well is the question method. I'll anticipate the questions that I think people will ask and then I'll write down the answers as the basis for my speech. You can incorporate the questions themselves into your speech or even display them on a PowerPoint or you can simply use them as a framework for your speech. Building your speech around anticipated questions will give a natural order and flow to your speech.

The few times that I had reservations about performing in a particular show were times when I wasn't fully prepared. Perhaps I didn't take the time to gather some background information on the group I was working for, or ask around about the peculiarities of the town where I was performing. Whatever the reason, the truth is I just wasn't prepared to do those shows. They were the shows that made me most nervous. Knowing your material and having something up your sleeve about your crowd will give you the confidence to deliver a memorable speech.

Make eye contact with your audience. Select a couple of people scattered throughout the crowd and look at them as if you were talking to them directly. This eye contact will make the audience feel welcome and important. It also contributes to your credibility and sincerity as a speaker.

If you want to improve your speaking with very little effort, take time to observe other public speakers. Take notes on things you liked and disliked, not on what they said but how they said it. Think of an educator, a minister, a politician, someone who made a big impression on your life. What did they do that was so special? Why were they able to make a connection with their audience? Did they use humor?

When you are sitting in an audience, jot down aspects of the performer's routine that worked for you and try to incorporate these same things into your work. Ask yourself, "What type of presentation would I want to sit through? What would I do differently?"

One way to get your creative juices flowing is to go to a comedy club on an open-stage night when comedians are trying new material. Often the comedians will use a generic funny line (in the business, this is called as a "stock joke") when one of their new jokes fails to get the desired laugh. Make a mental note of the phrase and add it to your collection. The lines these guys use have been in the public domain for years and are passed down from comedian to comedian. If you hear a joke you'd like to use in your presentation, make sure to credit the comedian. You don't want to be accused of stealing material.

Have a few lines or funny quips ready to use if something goes wrong. These are fall-back responses that are completely in the can but will seem like off-the-cuff remarks to the crowd. For example, if you are using visual aids and a photo is upside down, you could say, "I guess my daughter was on the computer last night." Or if a joke falls flat, you could use one of my favorite go-to lines: "You know, folks, last week I was in Las Vegas, entertainment capital of the world, and apparently I did so well there that this week I'm *here*!"

I hope these little nuggets get you thinking about how you can spice up your speech or presentation. More importantly, I hope they get you thinking about what your audience needs and wants.

OVERCOMING FEAR

"According to most studies, people's number one fear is public speaking. Death is number two.... That means to the average person, if you go to a funeral, you're better off in the casket than doing the eulogy."

—Jerry Seinfeld

A t some point in your life you are going to have to address a group of people. It could be at a wedding, a retirement party, or even a wake. It can be helpful to understand that most of the people in the crowd don't want to be out front. They appreciate what you are doing because most of them are thinking, "Better him than me." Once you take the stage, before you even open your mouth, you have their respect and admiration. You can take the stage with confidence because even if you flub a line or stumble on your words, no one is going to care. The only person there who wants the presentation to go perfectly is you. Your audience understands and will look past miscues. Most of them will feel for you if you screw up. They don't expect perfection. The only thing that should concern you is whether your audience will take something away from your talk.

My favorite book when I was a kid was a *Sesame Street* book featuring one of my favorite Muppets. The book was called *The Monster at the End of This Book,* and Grover was on the cover inviting you into the story. And yet, after every page you turned, Grover implored the reader to *not* turn the page. My mother read this story to me hundreds of times. There is a wonderful, wonderful build-up of suspense in the book. I loved it. Naturally you kept turning the pages and eventually you got to the end of the book. Grover pleads, "Please do not turn the page. Please. Please. Please." And it turned out that when you flipped the last page of the book, the monster actually was—Grover! He was the monster at the end of the book. There is a simple lesson here. And it's the first lesson you should learn. *Don't be afraid of being afraid.*

Some people seem to have a natural ability to talk in front of a crowd. There's no doubt about that. But the reason other people appear to be comfortable addressing a crowd is that they've done it before. Several times before. And they've seen several types of crowds before. It comes down to practicing. In order to develop any skill, you must repeat something again and again and again. There are those people who will speak in front of a crowd for the first time, have a bad experience, and never do it again. They never give themselves the chance to develop the skills to become a better speaker. As a matter of fact the most important advice I ever received as a comedian was from Jay Leno who told me, "Get on the stage as much as you can, wherever you can."

Tony Robbins said it years ago: repetition is the mother of skill. It's like in a basketball game when a player has to make a three-point shot to win the game. The coach wants the ball in the hands of the guy who takes that shot every day in practice. You're going to get the ball to Michael Jordan. You have to do something enough to become comfortable with it. It's just that simple. Nike has the best slogan for anybody who needs to speak in front of a crowd – *Just do it.*

Considering how important it is to speak in front of an audience in business, I can't believe that people don't work on it more often. I have seen so many executives, important executives, who are unable to address an audience effectively, and it drives me nuts. In their line of work, speaking is so important, yet they apparently spend little time developing the skills they need to become effective speakers. I'm going to tell you right now, you can read all the books you want about speaking, but reading a book is not going to make you a better speaker. If you want to be good at speaking in front of a crowd, you have to do it. Then you have to do it again, and then again. And you need a live crowd to do it. You can talk all you want in front of your bedroom mirror. You can tape yourself as many times as you want. But it's not the same as being in front of a crowd. The only thing that will help you, and I mean the only thing, is to speak in front of a crowd as often as you can. It's as simple as that. It really is.

It has been suggested that one way to alleviate the fear of public speaking is to imagine the crowd naked. Let me set the record straight. I once did a show at a nudist colony. I would have been better off imagining the people in their underwear. When you go to a nudist colony, it's not like going to the Playboy mansion. If it helps you to think of people nude, go for it. But I've been there and I'm not going back.

If you want to get better at public speaking, make every effort to get in front of a crowd as often as possible. If you're attending an event where someone has to address the crowd, volunteer to introduce the speaker. Elementary schools have vocational days when people from the community talk about their job. That's a great opportunity. Just because the audience is a group of twelve-year-olds, don't discount it. Some of these kids tend to be very uninhibited and ask questions that make you squirm and force you to think on your feet. Local charities have fundraising events that often need a person to host or emcee the program. What about joining Toastmasters International? This is an organization specifically designed to help members improve their communication skills. All of these activities will help desensitize you to speaking in public. You just have to get out there and do it.

CHOOSING
YOUR DELIVERY STYLE

*"It's not so much knowing
when to speak, it's knowing
when to pause."*

—Jack Benny

was lucky enough to meet the comedian Rocky Laporte backstage at a show. He's this normal guy, an ex-truck driver who
tells stories about his family and life. The first thing he says to
the crowd is, "How ya' doin'?" He comes off as just a regular
guy on stage. But that's an act. He's a really bright guy. Later on
he called me to talk about a booking agent, and he said, "You
know, Dave, this guy thinks I'm stupid." Rocky's delivery style
fits perfectly with how he looks on stage. His material reflects

his image as an average Joe. Rocky takes what people perceive him to be and builds a whole show around it. He's a really, really funny guy and his comedy is honest.

So what is your natural delivery or what character can you develop that fits the message you want to deliver? Is it a natural extension of your persona or is it an alter ego? It doesn't matter as long as the material that flows from you is in harmony with how you act and look on stage.

Writing jokes is not that easy. Sometimes it comes easy to you, but most of the time it's hard work. There are dozens of comedy-writing books that will take you step by step through the joke-writing process. They'll introduce you to the "formula." Now, I haven't read any of those books. I am self-taught. I don't think it's in your best interest for me to spend time teaching you how to write a joke. That's not what this book is about. The important thing is the *delivery* of the joke. You have to create your own style, particularly your own style of delivery. So even before you start writing material, you have to decide what your speech pattern or cadence is going to be.

There are probably a dozen or so comedic delivery styles. Eventually you will subscribe to one of them or close enough. But you have to decide. Are you a type like Steven Wright? Are you a type like Andrew Dice Clay? (Let's hope not. His style doesn't go over real well with the business crowd.) Is your style more like Dave Chappelle? George Carlin? Larry the Cable

Guy? But in deciding how you are going to deliver your material, you want to be thinking about your entire presentation, not just the funny stuff that you are going to do. The delivery style of your jokes has to mesh with the delivery style of the rest of your presentation.

For some people, it helps to pretend that you are someone else. Pretend you are playing a part in a play. It's funny to me how the same actors and actresses who win Academy awards for their flawless performances on screen become totally flustered when they come up in front of their peers to accept the award. The reason is simple: On screen, they are putting themselves into another body. They are becoming someone else. But when they are off screen, they are who they are and it's not always easy to just be yourself. I think that's at the root of the stage fright that comes with public speaking. You're worried about yourself and your shortcomings and what you perceive to be your shortcomings and whether you will reveal those shortcomings to your audience. But imagine that if you walk out there thinking you're the best speaker there ever was, you really truly believe it, then you're going to be the best speaker there ever was. It may only be in your mind, but there's nothing wrong with that. For the duration of the speech or presentation, you can allow yourself to become a different persona. Just make sure that the material you deliver along with the jokes fits with the persona you have chosen to become.

If you think there is any possibility that something you plan to say might be considered to be in bad taste, don't use it. In the corporate world, clean is always the way to go. Clean will open doors for you anywhere. You don't want to be locked out of a possible gig or crossed off a speakers list just because you can't work clean. If you work dirty you can work in a nightclub or a bar. Sometimes even nightclubs are reluctant to have dirty comedians.

Humor will always make any presentation more effective. However, you don't have to do a clown act to pull off a successful presentation. Everybody enjoys a good joke. It's a great way to break the ice. I don't want you to think that you have to be a comedian to be able to use this book. But you ought to think of yourself as an entertainer.

A lot of people are reluctant to add humor to their presentation. Many people think, "I'm not funny." You don't have to be funny. You're not doing a ten-minute monologue. All you have to do is tell a joke or a funny story. There is a difference. Sure, some people will have a better delivery or be a better storyteller. That's fine. You're just looking for that little boost that a joke or amusing anecdote can give your speech.

Very early in my comedy career I developed a friendship with another Pittsburgh-based comedian, Jimmy Krenn. Jimmy is not the most famous name on a national level but in Pittsburgh he's the biggest name in comedy. I had been performing professionally for about a year when Jimmy asked

CHOSING YOUR DELIVERY STYLE

me to open for him for a series of banquets. My job was to greet the crowd, tell a few jokes, and then introduce the main act—Jimmy. What was unique about Jimmy's set at that time was that he'd open with a standard joke-joke—the "three men walk into a bar. . ." type of joke—before delivering some fresh material. After a couple of shows I asked Jimmy why he did joke-jokes, because most comedians stay away from them. He told me, "That's what they want to hear. They're used to these kinds of jokes. And they can go back to the office and tell that joke easier than they can do one of my impressions." Jimmy was giving the audience what they want and the audience was taking back something from his show to share with their friends. As a communicator, don't you want people to remember your words and share them with the world?

If you don't feel comfortable telling a joke yourself, there is an easy way to incorporate into your presentation, which is to show a joke via the PowerPoint. And if it doesn't work, you can blame the comedian telling the joke.

What if it doesn't work? If they don't laugh, so what? They didn't show up expecting a comedian. The crowd at a business presentation will forget about it in a minute or two. On the other hand, if a comedian goes on stage and doesn't get any laughs, then that's trouble.

We've all had teachers who spoke in a monotone or didn't do much besides scribble on the blackboard. Do you ever talk about those teachers? Do you say, "Wow, I really miss them…

they were fantastic. I learned so much from them." No, nobody says that about those people. That's because they never made a connection with anyone.

A lot of people don't want to take a risk by being funny or entertaining in their presentations, but believe me you need to be if you want to reach your audience. And it's not as big a risk as you think it is, especially when you are doing a presentation for the corporate world, for a college or high school crowd, for the Rotary Club. Why? The bar is lower for speakers than it is for professional entertainers and comedians. Still, if you can think of a speaker whose words stayed with you long after the speech was over, chances are the speech had some element of entertainment in it.

I had a high-school algebra teacher who always spoke in a monotone voice. She was a traditional nun in every sense, and it took everything I had to stay awake in class. But one day she came to class with a smile on her face. She asked us if we wanted to hear a joke. We did. She said, "What's 5Q plus 5Q?" Someone called out, "10Q." And she said, "You're welcome." She got a big laugh—not because it was a particularly funny joke but because telling a joke was out of character for her. Comedy is all about the unexpected. It's leading a person one way and then going off in a different direction. She told a bad joke but got a big laugh because we didn't expect it. Speakers can get away with telling a corny joke as well.

Nowadays comedians are more likely to talk about amusing events that happened in their life than to rattle off jokes from a standard repertoire. Everybody has funny stories. When families or friends get together, they often sit around and tell funny stories. You can use those stories in your presentation. Right now you may be saying to me, "Dave, they have nothing to do with my subject." Fair enough. I'm going to show you a technique that I use in my presentations that will let you interject funny stories in between blocks of material that will keep the audience entertained and enthused about your main subject. Sometimes you can find a way to tie them in, but it's not necessary—as long as you get back to your subject frequently enough so that your audience remembers what it is.

Years ago something not so funny happened in my life that I was able to turn into a funny story. My car was stolen. I woke up one day and went outside to get the paper and there was nothing but broken glass on the ground where my car had been parked. All I wanted to do that morning was read the paper over a cup of coffee—not deal with a stolen car.

It was the first time I'd ever had anything stolen. So I called the police department, and they said they'd let me know if the car turned up. Well, the next day they found my car. Apparently some kids were breaking into cars in the area and going out for joy rides. So my cousin and I went down to check out the car at the city pound. We looked inside and decided it didn't look too bad. I mean, the trunk was popped, a couple of windows were broken, the inside was kind of trashed, but over all it didn't look too bad. Then I opened the door and sat down inside. Immediately I was overtaken by "the smell." It was body odor, and it was horrific. I thought I was going to gag. I got out of the car immediately and my cousin laughed. The odor was so bad it was funny. Who has BO bad enough to have it permeate a car?

I had the car towed to my garage and the insurance guy came out to look at it. He walked around the car, looking at the front and back and made a few notes. He didn't see anything that looked really bad. No major damage. Then he opened the door, sat down in the car, got a whiff of the odor, gasped, grabbed his clipboard, and wrote—TOTALED.

So how does someone integrate a story like this into a speech or presentation? It's simple. In my case, I simply ask the crowd how their day is going or if they are having a good week. And then I say, "Not me. I had my car stolen the other day." Then I tell them the story. It's a great way to get your audience to relax, but it also helps *you* to relax. And then you can launch into your speech or presentation.

The best thing about the Totaled joke was that it took on a life of its own. A good friend of mine was a writer for *The Dennis Miller Show.* On most television shows, the writers' room is a collection of warm bodies, fast-food wrappers, and boxes of day-old pizza. It's an olfactory nightmare. My friend told Dennis the Totaled joke and he got a kick out of it. From that point on, when one of the writers hadn't showered, everyone else in the room would just wink at each other and say, "TOTALED." Coincidentally, there was a *Seinfeld* episode a couple of years later that also featured a stinky car.

So you never know when an event from your life can be fodder for a joke. Keep track of the funny things that happen to you at home, at work, on the road. Write them down. You can always embellish them to make them even funnier. Comedians are known for scribbling stuff on anything they can find—the back of a deposit slip, an envelope, a gum wrapper. Some carry a tape recorder with them. You'll want to make a note of anything that you think is even remotely funny. As you do this more and more, your comedic antennae will start picking up funnier and funnier bits. Once you start thinking like a comedian you'll eventually start writing like a comedian.

One of my favorite speakers is Christine Cashen. She does a wonderful job of splicing in humorous stories about her life throughout her talks. She is not a trained comedian, but her jokes help her to get important points across to her audience. I once attended an all-day conference in which Christine had the after-lunch time slot. That is a tough time to be on stage. Typically the crowd filters in as you begin your presentation and then partway into your talk the attendees start dozing off as they crash from their carb intake. Christine understood what she was facing and did something brilliant. She started off with a song called the "Boogie Dance," which required the crowd to get out of their seats and join in a business-themed dance. Some of the people were a little self-conscious and reluctant at first, but eventually she had everyone dancing. Christine got them to start communicating with her and got their brains functioning. What's more, she got them laughing and enjoying themselves, even before she started her performance. She had them before she even said hello.

If you don't feel confident enough about your own material, have a backup plan. Most comedians write jokes with the expectation that people will laugh at them. I do that, but I take it one step further. After I write a joke I write another joke that can be waiting in the wings. It's called a throwaway line in our business. How it works is that if people don't laugh at your joke, you have another joke that makes fun of how bad the previous joke was or you make a comment about the crowd not laughing at the joke. If you have a back-up line, you'll have more confidence to try a new joke, knowing that if it doesn't go over well, you have a safety net.

Let me give you an example of a throwaway line. If I'm speaking to a corporate crowd and three or four of my jokes in a row don't go too well, I'll say, "You know what, folks? I don't care if you laugh or not, I'm not even a comedian; however, I did stay at a Holiday Inn Express last night." What that does is engage the audience with a subtle piece of comedy.

Years ago, a comedian friend of mine, Augie Cook, came up to me after a particularly challenging show and said, "You know what, buddy? You die better than anyone I've ever seen." He was talking about my throwaway lines. I love working tough crowds. Why? Because a tough audience is a true measure of how good you are, how quick you are on your feet. Throwaway lines are powerful and effective tools for me. I believe in them, and I use them a lot in my presentations. Of course, you can decide whether or not you think they'd work for you too.

LIGHTS,
CAMERA, ACTION

"There is no business like show business, but there are several businesses like accounting."
—David Letterman

Before the best comedians work a new venue, they always take inventory of their surroundings. You should too. First you want to take notice of how the room is set up. How are the chairs and tables arranged? Will there be people with their back to you? Are there any obstructions between you and the audience? I was working a room once that had a series of huge columns running down each aisle. As I moved back and forth across the stage, the people seated behind the columns had to lean to the left and then to the right to see me. I shortly figured out that I had to stand in the middle of the stage.

Some rooms are just designed better than others for speaking to an audience. They have a good feel. If the space seems too big, you will have to make an extra effort to create intimacy. You can bring the crowd closer to the stage. You can interact with the audience by asking a few questions. Big rooms need more energy from the speaker. It is easier to connect with people in a small room simply because they are physically closer to you.

The comfort level of the audience can affect the quality of the show. Being packed in like sardines has a negative effect on people and fosters a sense of anonymity and distance from the speaker. If the audience is spread all over the room or there are big gaps in the crowd, suggesting sparse attendance, attendees may find themselves questioning the credibility of the presenter. You want to be clear with the people hosting the event that they fill the seats at the front of the room first. Ideally you want the room filled but not crowded.

You'll want to check the stage, walk across it a few times. There could be a ripple in the carpet that you could catch a toe on. There could be spots that are bouncy. Who knows? The thing is, you don't want to be caught by surprise during your presentation. Of course, you can't control all the things that could go wrong. It could be something as crazy as a streaker running across the stage or as simple as dropping the microphone. If something unexpected happens, you need to be able to work with it. You need to be able to make fun of yourself or the particular plight you're in, and work with it. This is where you will draw from the repertoire of funny quips and asides that you picked up at the comedy club.

You'll want to check the lighting and audio equipment. There's nothing worse than a poor sound system. You are better off projecting your voice than using a system that fades in and out or that crackles. Will you be using a handheld microphone or a clip-on? Is it a cordless mic? What about the batteries? I always travel with a spare microphone and extra batteries. Stay away from podiums with built-in microphones, if you can. I have yet to find a built-in microphone that produces a decent sound quality. If you are using PowerPoint, you'll want to make sure that it is running properly. What about the quality of the projector? Will the people in the back row be able to read the fine print on the screen? If you are working in the afternoon, could natural light coming in through the windows cause a glare or wash out the images on the screen? You want to be in control in as much of your environment as possible. Don't leave anything to chance.

Another thing to consider is your wardrobe. You bring your favorite red dress to wear. The only problem is, the curtain behind the stage is the exact same color. When you take the stage you blend into the background. Always bring some back-up clothing. You never know, what if you spill a drink on your pants?

I always wear a suit, whether it's a comedy show or a business engagement. I'm not trying to out-dress people. I like the idea of what a suit projects. I think it lends to my credibility and gives me a head start on earning the crowd's respect.

For your convenience I've assembled a pre-show checklist:

PRE-SHOW CHECKLIST

- ☐ Layout of room/Seating
- ☐ Stage
- ☐ Microphone
- ☐ Batteries
- ☐ AV / Power point equipment
- ☐ Pointer / Laser
- ☐ Wardrobe
- ☐ Grooming / Appearance
- ☐ Glass of water
- ☐ Note cards

Once you've taken stock of the room, it's now time to visualize your performance in that space. Find a quiet area and rehearse your speech.

You'll want to keep in mind the elements of the room and how can you use them to enhance your speech. Early in my career I worked a bar in a bowling alley. It had a pallet for a stage that was lit by a construction work lamp. Every time someone left the bar to enter the bowling alley you could hear pins crashing in the background. Not an ideal performing venue. Instead of ignoring the situation I made fun of it. Everyone in the room knew the circumstances. My thoughts were, "Let's acknowledge it. Make fun of it and move on." I remember saying something like, "You know you've made it when you're working a bowling alley in Greensburg, PA!" It turned out to be a good show. Had I ignored the bad lighting and makeshift stage the crowd might have thought I was used to this sort of venue. At the very least, they would have wondered why I didn't comment on the noise or the ridiculous set-up.

I had the honor of opening for Howie Mandel at the Amphitheater in Pittsburgh's Station Square. This amphitheater is probably the most difficult outdoor venue to work in the country. Usually these types of venues are located in quiet areas that are conducive to concerts. Not in Pittsburgh. The place is sandwiched between the Monongahela River and a cliff face. It gets worse. There's a busy highway at the foot of the cliff, and running parallel to the river are two sets of railroad tracks. About every twenty minutes a train rumbles past the stage, maybe fifty feet away at best!

Soon after Howie's limo dropped him off, we were backstage exchanging pleasantries when a train passed by. I wish I had had a camera with me to catch the expression on his face. He looked at me and asked, "These trains will stop, right?" I shrugged my shoulders. "Not unless there's a wreck!" Howie shook his head and said, "You've got to be kidding me. That's going to be going on all night?"

So we put our heads together and started tossing ideas around about how we could pull off a show under these circumstances. We had to go through our material and figure out what jokes would work and, more importantly, prepare for the pauses we would have to build into our act whenever a train passed by. It's not like you get interrupted for a few seconds—some of the trains take a minute or two to pass. This will ruin any flow or momentum you have established as a performer.

Howie, true professional that he is, took what looked like an impossible situation and made it work. The first time a train passed, Howie made fun of his agent for booking him in a railyard. He then went on to poke fun at the engineer and used the down time to do his trademark rubber glove bit. The show could have been a disaster, but we focused on adapting our material, anticipated the problems that would arise, made light of our predicament, and like the trains, moved on.

Another show comes to mind that illustrates how you cannot prepare for every situation. I was asked to emcee a student-faculty basketball game. My job was to provide running commentary during the game and perform a comedy show at halftime. I was a few minutes into the halftime program when a loud buzzer sounded. I didn't think anything about it until it happened again. And then again. It was then that I realized that the student running the scoreboard had taken it upon himself to sound the buzzer any time he didn't approve of one of my jokes. The audience thought it was hilarious. I wanted to choke the kid. Suppressing the urge to run over and knock him off his chair, I just went with the flow. The next time he hit the buzzer, I said, "It's pretty sad when a buzzer gets more laughs than the comedian."

You can control a lot of things, but you can't control everything. Be as prepared as you can by going through your checklist and arming yourself with a few prepared lines that we talked about in the Getting Started chapter.

Once you've taken inventory of the room your next job is to review the audience. The ability to assess a crowd is invaluable to comedians and can pay big dividends for a public speaker. You have to be able judge the general tenor of the crowd. Are these people attentive, anxious, bored, tired? How do you do this? The bad news is, I can't teach it to you in a book. The good news is, it's a skill that can be learned. The best way to acquire this skill is to speak dozens of times in front of different types of audiences. It will take you a while, but it's worth it. A good way to accelerate this process is to be more observant of the audience when you attend any public gathering. Keep your antennae working all the time. Scan the crowd and make a broad appraisal of their energy and attentiveness. Now look for individuals who might carry some weight in the crowd. Those are the people who you'll want to make eye contact with when you are on stage.

Becoming an audience expert will elevate your ability to communicate your message and deliver a memorable presentation.

MY FIRST BIG WEEK...
working one of the most prestigious chains, The Improv

PLAYING BIG SHOT on a movie set

AND THE WINNER IS...
goofing off with a friend's awards

MY GOOD FRIEND

Rocky Laporte with me in a really
bad "comedy-condo"

BACKSTAGE PASS

from opening with Michael Bolton

June 21, 1991

Dear David:

Enclosed herewith is an independent contractors
agreement. I would appreciate it greatly if you would
sign this and return it to me in the return envelope
provided for your convenience. Please retain a copy
for your files.

Thank you for all of your assistance.

Cordially yours,

Helen G. Kushnick

Enclosures

My first big contract

signing with Jay Leno's legendary manager Helen Kushnick

JIM KRENN AND I

on the night of our first national television appearance

At a recent engagement
with my good friend Tom Anzalone, Mr. Songflower Man

Frank Nicotero
with me at one of our annual holiday shows

LESS IS MORE

*"It is better to leave your
audience before your
audience leaves you."*
—**Anonymous**

❝Thank you, good night! I'll be here all week. Try the veal."
Comedians use that line all the time. Basically, it's a way to
get off the stage on a **high note**. The concept even made
its way onto a *Seinfeld* episode. Any time George Costanza had
a funny line and people laughed at it, he would say, "All right!
That's it for me. Goodnight, everybody." And then he'd walk out
of the room.

Knowing how and when to finish is extremely important. Some speakers or presenters have the crowd in the palm of their hand and then they go on a little longer and end up losing the crowd. Had they had said goodbye a few minutes earlier, the crowd might have thought, "That guy was great. I could see him again." Instead, they are thankful that he ended. The best compliment that you can get is to have audience members come up to you afterwards and say, "That was fantastic. I wished you had stayed up there longer." Always leave them wanting more.

It is very important to take notice of the crowd as you wrap up your presentation. You've delivered your message. The crowd is hanging on your every word. They are enjoying the moment. It's at that very moment that you need to make your exit—gracefully and quickly.

Know when to quit. It's never a good sign when you see people in your audience half-asleep or staring off into space.

A lot of speakers, including comedians, don't get it. They get too wrapped up in what they're doing up there and forget the audience. They may be getting a major ego stroke by being the center of attention and getting laughs or giving a good presentation, or maybe they just like to hear themselves talk. I don't know how many times I've seen comedians make the mistake of not gauging the audience correctly. If you concentrate more on your audience and less on yourself, you'll be a more effective speaker. It really is all about the audience, it's not about you. "Less is more" is for their benefit as well as your own. You always want to leave them wanting more. If you think you are talking too long, you probably are.

Elvis, one of the greatest showmen of all time, never did an encore. And there's a reason why. Elvis knew he gave his all on stage and made sure the crowd got their money's worth. So when he was done, he was done, and he left the stage. His announcer would take the microphone and say, "Elvis has left the building." It was his way of letting the crowd know that the King was not coming back. Elvis's fans would not leave the building until they were sure the show was over. Elvis always left them wanting more.

There are several other reasons why you should keep your presentation short. Chances are, you think that what you have to say is important and you want to share as much of your knowledge as you can. But it's not what you know that's important. It's what your audience retains. You are better off building your speech or presentation around a few salient points that they can take home with them. The brain can only take in so much. A presenter rambling on for an hour or so is the equivalent of cramming for an exam. Research has shown that cramming for a test is ineffective because the subject matter that you are cramming into your head will not be retained. Cramming causes students to confuse facts and it prohibits the brain from processing the information. This is not what you want. You want attentive listeners waiting for your next nugget of wisdom.

This doesn't mean giving your audience three-fourths of a presentation or leaving out material. But you want to get your point across. The audience has to feel satiated. Cut out the fluff. Figure out your main points and beat your audience over the head with them. And then get off stage. You can always provide a brochure or a link to your Web site that features a more thorough explanation of your topic.

Another reason to keep it short is respect for your audience. Everyone appreciates a speaker, lecturer, or minister who gets his or her point across with a minimum of words. It's actually a relief to find someone who values your time as much as their own. To be honest with you, the most challenging task I had writing this book was whittling down the material. There are a lot of stories I wanted to share with you, but there is only a certain amount of information you need to know.

A good friend of mine, Frank Nicotero, has an Internet show called *Primetime in No Time*. Frank and I cut our teeth together on the national comedy circuit. Frank's show is a three-minute recap of the previous night's primetime shows. It's the most watched original video program in Internet history, with over 500 million streams. You know why? Because it's funny and it saves people time. Who can watch every primetime show on every channel every night? Frank can, it's his job. The rest of us just don't have time.

If you simply regurgitate your material verbatim or read your material from PowerPoint, you're cheating the audience worse than if you go a few minutes short. If you have some time to fill, you can always ask the audience if they have any questions. You should have a thorough understanding of your subject, and feel comfortable discussing it. If you're not sure of your answer, be honest. Fudging an answer will cause an audience to doubt your credibility more than telling them you just don't know.

One way to connect with an audience is to throw out a couple of questions. It can be as simple as, "Anyone celebrating a birthday today?" or "Anyone from out of town?" You can also ask for a volunteer to come on stage. You can quiz them about the subject you are speaking on or ask them what they expect to gain from today's experience, or what they've done at the convention so far. You're not bringing them up to embarrass them. The last thing you want to do is bring an audience member onstage and embarrass them. Just like a good lawyer, you never ask a question that you do not already have an answer for. This is how you work the crowd. Do comedians get surprised or stumped by an audience member? Sure it happens, but most of the time we have a reply or a retort ready to go. When I get surprised, I acknowledge the person and tell them, "Wow, I've been doing this for twenty-five years and that's the first time I've ever heard that answer. Am I in the right room? I didn't accidentally walk into an Amway meeting, did I?" That usually gets a laugh and I move on.

You want to set the tone so that the audience will begin concentrating enough that they will be receptive to the main points you want to get across. But in between making those points, you ought to be entertaining your audience. This is how I do it: If my allotted time is forty minutes, it usually takes me about half that time to get my points across. I spend the first five minutes greeting and warming up the crowd. The next five minutes I introduce the major points of my presentation. Then I entertain the crowd for the next five minutes followed by another five minutes devoted to reviewing my big points. Halfway through the presentation I might take a few minutes of questions from the crowd. This will depend on my read of the audience. If I think they are drifting off, I'll hit them up with some questions. If I think I have them in my hands, I'll work the crowd a little bit and then hit my points again, probably giving the audience some type of mnemonic device to help them take home what I want them to remember. (O. J. Simpson's attorney, Johnny Cochran, whittled his case down to the famous line "If the glove doesn't fit, you must acquit." That resonated with the jury more than all the hours of testimony by the experts and the witnesses.) In the last five minutes I go into my close, which I have tailored to this specific audience. Maybe I'll say, "Thank you. Good night. I'll be here all week. Try the veal." Maybe not. But you get my point.

WORKING THE ROOM

> "*Comedians walk out, get a feel for the crowd. If it's not going well, we change directions— if we have to drag your momma into this thing, we will.... Whatever we got to do.*"
> —**Steve Harvey**

teve Harvey taught me a lot about working the crowd. It's a rush. If you become comfortable interacting with the audience, you will never have an off day. No matter how dire the situation—your microphone acts up, you can't access your PowerPoint—no problem. You can use these setbacks to your advantage. Work the crowd and get them on your side.

I learned early on in my comedy career that each audience is different. I could do a set and have the crowd going crazy. The next night I could do the same jokes and struggle to get a laugh.

One of the things that never failed was working the room. This isn't anything new. It was probably used around the campfire by cavemen. I can tell you that the success rate of working the room, when done correctly, is so high that most comedians think it's cheating.

Now when I say cheating, I don't mean on an ethical level. Some of the comedic purists think that you should be able to go onstage, and solely on the basis of the delivery of your material, get laughs. That works most of the time if you have a good crowd. You don't always have that option. By working the room, you force a crowd that is unresponsive to listen to you. Once you begin asking questions, everyone in the audience will take notice because nobody wants to look foolish in front of their peers. They'll get anxious because you are in the crowd talking to them. You're going to get a lot of nervous laughter. But what you are really doing is creating excitement. You are keeping the audience on their toes.

Let's be honest, when you don't work the room, the audience can do whatever they want—sit back, relax, take a nap, text a friend, scroll their Blackberry. They don't have to listen to you. No one's forcing them to. You're up front, and they're settled in their seats. When you begin to ask them questions, you are drawing the audience in with you. You are breaking the fourth wall.

The term "fourth wall" comes from the theater. In a typical, staged theater show there are three visible walls. An invisible fourth wall exists between the actors and the audience. When actors speak directly to the audience, they are said to be breaking the fourth wall. It's no longer you on stage and them in the crowd. You are becoming one of them.

Many people think that if they sit up front, the comedian is going to pick on them. I've been a comedian for twenty-five years and that's not necessarily the case. Sure, you will find the occasional comedian who will pick on someone in the crowd, especially if that person is being disruptive. In that case, the heckler is getting what he deserves. Fans have asked me why comedians single out members of the audience and poke fun at them. The answer is, because it works. When a comedian is struggling to get a laugh, it's an easy way to get a few chuckles. But it has to be done in the right spirit. Good-natured ribbing goes over a lot better than ridicule. Be sensitive to the difference.

So what does it take to work a room? You have to be prepared in a couple of ways. You have to know your material inside and out. You have to be ready to deal with the unexpected. And, perhaps most importantly, you have to know how to read your audience.

That means doing research on the crowd you will be facing. Your life will be a lot easier if you know the general background of the audience. Say it's a corporate gig; you'll want to know what the company does, what products it sells. If you're new to the town where you are making your presentation, find out about it. One of the best at this is Jay Leno. Not only does Jay do three hundred TV shows a year, but he still goes on the road, working comedy clubs and doing speaking engagements. When Jay arrives in town to do a show, he makes a point of finding out something about the history of the town, or what it's known for. Sometimes he'll visit the town's hot spots or places where the locals hang out. He will open his show with seven to ten minutes of material specifically targeted to that town. He might make fun of the town in a light-hearted way, but that makes a connection with the crowd. He creates a shared experience that endears him to the audience. Once he has established that bond, he is free to take the crowd anywhere he wants to go because the audience is completely with him. This is the essence of working the room, and it is what makes each show unique.

Years ago I worked a Dapper Dan sports banquet in Pittsburgh, an annual event that honors Western Pennsylvania's high school, college, and professional athletes. It's a big deal in Pittsburgh because it always draws some big names from the sports world. I was asked by the committee to add a little entertainment to the program. That particular evening featured Jaromir Jagr, Joe Paterno, and Bill Cowher. I had prepared a few minutes of generic, sports-related material and had no intention of going to the crowd that evening. Having done a little prep work by finding out who would be on the dais that evening, I was able to compose a few lines for some of the guests. About halfway through my material I made a joke about the

Steelers. A guy in the front row said, "Oooh… making fun of Coach Cowher." Now I was at the podium and Bill Cowher was sitting right next to me. I couldn't quite see him out of the corner of my eye. So then I said, "You mean the Jay Leno of the football world?" (Coach Cowher is known for his strong jaw line.) That got a half-decent response and I said to the guy in the front row, "Is he laughing? Please tell me he's laughing! 'Cause I sure wouldn't want to fight him—he spits harder than I punch!" With that line the entire audience erupted in laughter. It was well known that when Cowher yelled at people, spit would fly out of his mouth. The fact that Cowher laughed too, even though he was the butt of a joke, helped me connect with my audience. The following day that line made it into the local papers. I had phone calls from people wanting to book me for their events.

Now I'll let you in on a little secret. When I was doing my prep work for the show, I composed a few lines about Cowher and his volatile personality. One of the lines was about how he can spit harder than I punch. Luckily, I picked the one line that worked perfectly for that situation and that audience. But it looked to everyone as though I had thought up that line on the spot. That's another secret from the comedy world—improvisation is not always what it seems. When you see so-called improv skits, rarely are the performers truly improvising. Most of the time the funny lines that they come up with have been stored in their heads and they are simply recalling them for the appropriate situation.

I was talking to a few audience members after one of my performances and they brought up the Drew Carey TV show, *Whose Line Is It Anyway*. They were disheartened to find out that most of what appears to be ad-libbed on the show is actually scripted. My response was, "Do you really think Wayne Brady is able to compose an entire song on the spot?" To me it seemed so evident that the program was planned out ahead of time. The magic of the show is that it looked like the performers were thinking up those funny lines on the spot. There's an extremely powerful effect on the audience when you can pull off improvisation. They think you are smart, clever, and most importantly, entertaining. This makes them hang onto your every word. And isn't that what you want when you are speaking to a crowd?

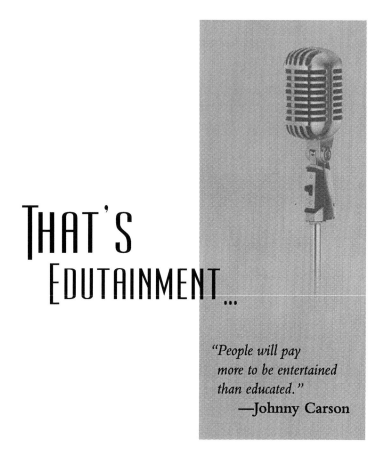

THAT'S
EDUTAINMENT...

There is nothing like the feeling you get from making a group of people laugh. I remember the first time I was able to get laughs on stage as a comedian. It was one of the most exhilarating experiences of my life. As time went on, it didn't matter if I was in a smoke-filled bar or a fancy concert hall, the feeling was the same. You get a sense of love and adulation, but it's the power you feel you have over the audience that's intoxicating. Once you have their trust, you can try out new material and even push the envelope a bit. You can take them wherever you want to go. The same is true for all speakers. If you can be entertaining, the chances of reaching your audience are infinitely better.

There's actually a word for this: edutainment. Obviously, it's the combination of education and entertainment. When I first heard this term I thought, "Hey, I've been doing this for years." Edutainment is becoming more pervasive in the educational world, but little has been done regarding presentations and speech making. Nevertheless, it's predicted that an entire industry will develop around edutainment. That's a big deal. As more and more educators use edutainment in their classrooms their students will become conditioned to learn that way. As these students grow older they will also expect future learning experiences to be edutainment-based. If you are not entertaining while you are trying to get your subject matter across to your audience, they may not listen to your words.

The mix of educating, entertaining and humor has been a part of learning for some time; you probably didn't even realize it. I can remember back to my youth and it still resonates with me 30 years later. Now the subject matter wasn't something that I was particularly interested in, but the message was packaged in such a way that the information still rattles around in my head. I'm talking about *Schoolhouse Rock!*

When people hear the words "conjunction junction what's your function?" or "I'm just a bill" they immediately recall Saturday morning cartoon images and those catchy songs that have never left them. Do you think it's a coincidence that the man responsible for the *Schoolhouse Rock!* concept came from advertising? When you are teaching or presenting at a seminar or anytime you're in front of an audience you want them to remember your message. *Schoolhouse Rock!* first aired in the 1970's and there's a whole generation that can recite the lyrics to those animations thirty years later. That's pretty powerful.

Many of the TV programs geared toward children—*Sesame Street, Electric Company, The Muppet Show,* and the shows of today like *Super Why, Word World, Sid the Science Kid*—combine entertainment and education. *The Muppet Show* is particularly endearing to me because of Fozzie Bear, the character that wants to be a comedian. Many times during my career I've seen two old guys in the audience and immediately had visions of the two old guys that heckle Fozzie. I usually tell them they remind me of the guys from *The Muppet Show* and that gets a lot of laughs. This goes to show you the popularity of these shows *and* how a rehearsed "improvisational" line can work.

The latest generation of audiences has been conditioned to learn a different way because of television. They are used to getting their information packaged in the form of entertainment. I believe this is the most important aspect of an audience that a speaker can be aware of. If you want to be an effective speaker, you must accept this fact and add edutainment to your presentation. Crowds today have grown up with *Schoolhouse Rock!*, twenty-four-hour comedy networks, *YouTube*, and funny ads that people talk about over the water cooler. Kids do their homework while listening to their iPod. They expect a little spice. Give it to them, whether it's a joke, a prop, music, or even a little magic. It's all edutainment.

GUITARS,
MUSIC, AND PROPS

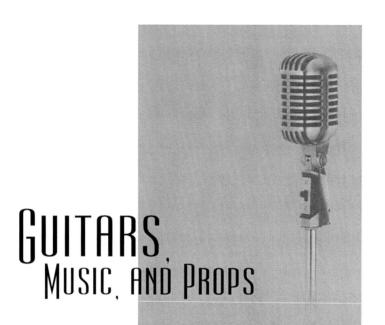

"No matter what you have going on in your life, if you are able to laugh you are able to forget about it for a second or two."
—**Red Skelton**

I rarely use prop materials in my act, though I've worked with a lot of comedians who use them all the time. I've worked with talented musicians who specialize in song parodies and even the occasional ventriloquist. One ventriloquist act, *Otto and George*, was so convincing that after a show an audience member tried to stab George, the dummy. That's one powerful presentation. The fact that a performer could stir that much feeling from an audience member is amazing. I have to be honest with you.

The first time I performed with Otto and George, I actually said after the show, "You two were great!"

When I was just starting out as a comedian, I happened to bump into Red Skelton on my way to a comedy club. One of the all-time greats, he was in Pittsburgh to receive an award. I got to spend about ten minutes with him. We chatted about the comedy business, and I asked him if he had any advice for me. There he was, now confined to a wheelchair but still sporting a flamboyant necktie. He smiled at me, ruffled his tie, flipped it up in the air, and said, "Props." Then he tipped his hat and off he went.

To be honest, I had never really considered using props in my act, partly because I didn't want to lug around a lot of stuff from show to show. Besides, I believed that I could get people to laugh through my words and facial expressions. There are people in the comedy world who look down on magicians, clowns, and ventriloquists because they use props. These comedians are of the opinion that it's copping out, that using a prop is an easy way to get a laugh. It's tantamount to cheating. Well, folks, it's not cheating. People love prop acts. Carrot Top has his own show in Las Vegas. Weird Al Yankovic won an Emmy. *Jeff Dunham and Peanut* is one of the top acts in the country, reportedly earning over $30 million one year. Sometimes it does take a little more than words to move a crowd. You may have to go to a visual or audio aid.

Enhancing your speech with a prop of some sort can make the difference between a bland lecture and a memorable performance. So now you may be thinking, what are my options? You can go the Los Angeles Lakers route and have a smoke machine and a laser-and-light show as you take the stage. Everyone will remember that. The problem is you want them to remember what you *said*, not what you did.

These days almost everyone has access to PowerPoint. It can be a very useful tool, a great prop. But it should only be a tool. If a presenter stands in front of the crowd and simply goes through his slides one after another, he's going to put the audience to sleep. Many people use PowerPoint to convey all of their boring, mind-numbing information. What a mistake! Think about that. You've just taken all of the material that you know is dull and put it together in one format and projected it onto a twenty-foot screen! Used correctly, PowerPoint can lift your presentation. You can use it to drive home your main points. Or use it to deliver funny material that you may not feel comfortable doing onstage. This is a great way to start to incorporate entertainment into your presentation. The thing to remember about PowerPoint is not to over-use it. You want to use PowerPoint to highlight your salient points and entertain your audience.

There are hundreds of ways to use PowerPoint to bring life to your material. When I'm doing a show for a company, I collect bits of information about the company and management staff, as well as some photos of employees. I'll take this info and transform it into a *Saturday Night Live* "Weekend Update"-type sketch. This works well because most of the people in the room know the people they see on the screen. Of course, I want to make sure that I'm not touching on any taboo or sensitive subject, so before the show I give a copy of the script to the people who will be cutting the check. You definitely don't want those people mad at you.

I was at a wedding and one of the groomsmen did a PowerPoint presentation at the reception. Now this guy was not a comedian, but you could tell he's a funny guy. He put on one of the best presentations I've ever seen. He had pictures of the bride and groom from various stages in their lives—from their baby photos up to just a few days before the wedding. He was basically telling the story of their lives. There were cute pictures, funny ones, ridiculous ones, embarrassing ones, you get the picture. Each photo had a caption and was woven into the storyline. It was really powerful, partly because the storyline was so well written and presented but also because the entire audience knew the characters on screen. This is a perfect example of how to make a connection with your crowd. Your chances for success improve dramatically if you gather a little background information and incorporate it into your presentation.

What if you could sum up your presentation in a song? Music makes a direct connection to a person's heart, mind, and body. When you hear a favorite song, it conjures up old memories, tugs at your heart, or makes you move your feet. Imagine if you ended your presentation with a three-minute ditty that had the audience singing your words as they left the building. Song parodies are an easy way to connect to a crowd. All you have to do is make a few of the lyrics related specifically to your audience. Heck, Weird Al has made a career out of this.

If an original musical production is beyond your reach, how about incorporating a sound track for your presentation or even using short cuts from popular songs to reinforce your message? What about a movie clip to illustrate a point?

I'm sure there are readers out there thinking, "Props are great for entertainers, but there's no place for them in business." Jim Cramer's *Mad Money* show on CNBC is a prime example of how props can be effectively incorporated into otherwise heavy-duty material. Cramer sets himself apart from the other financial talking heads by throwing chairs, punctuating stock opinions by using sound effects, and integrating catch phrases into his shtick. His ability to differentiate himself from other financial advisors has led to a career as a bestselling author and a popular personality on the college lecture circuit. When he spoke at Penn State, over fifteen thousand people showed up for the taping of his show. Jim Cramer was so connected with these college students that he got a rock-star welcome. The kids were screaming and cheering during the show. They even did the wave. It was a huge event on campus. This guy took a dry subject—the stock market—and by adding props made it a brilliant example of the power of edutainment.

TC Hatter, a professional circus clown who made the switch to stand-up comedy, used props in a way that really pushed the envelope. He'd take the stage dressed as a clown—along with his wife who came on toting a clarinet. If you think that sounds a bit off, well, TC took it another step. He did not speak on stage. He did his entire act, roughly 45 minutes to an hour, without talking to the crowd. He'd use facial expressions, body language, and props like the clarinet to communicate to the audience. And he was great. He got tons of laughs.

This is the best example that I can give you about how effective props can be. The first time I worked with TC I was blown away. I had always thought that a comedian's words were far and away the best way to communicate to the audience. After that night I learned the impact of props and music. TC Hatter can entertain a crowd without saying a word. How much more of an effective communicator do you think you can be if you add some music or props to your presentation?

Could you create a character that would help sell your message? Bob Newhart has been able to portray multiple characters by himself, simply by using words and mannerisms. Bill Cosby created characters by changing his expressions and altering his voice. In some cases, using an alter ego might help you to get your point across. But whatever you do, don't become a cartoon character, or get too gimmicky. There is a fine line.

After years on the comedy circuit Tom Anzalone developed an alter ego—Mr. Songflower Man. He goes to elementary schools where he passes his love of singing onto the children. He uses classic rock songs and traditional children's songs to engage students to sing along. What the kids don't know is that Tom is actually teaching them something called phonological awareness. He's teaching the young students how to recognize, arrange, and control small pieces of sound to form syllables, words and eventually sentences. He uses rhymes and jingles as a form of word play to help build language fluency. He makes it fun and enjoyable. He entertains them. He educates them. It's edutainment.

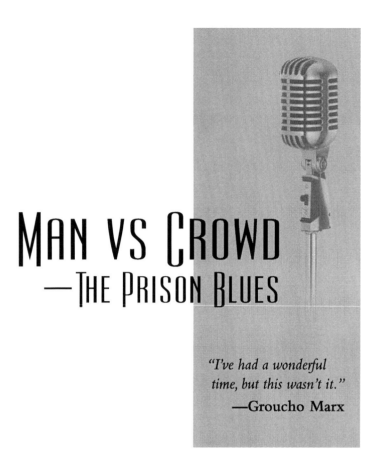

MAN VS CROWD
—THE PRISON BLUES

"I've had a wonderful time, but this wasn't it."
—Groucho Marx

've done time in ten different prisons. It's not what you think. My agent had a special gig lined up for me. Would I be willing to do ten shows over seven days at prisons scattered across Pennsylvania? The shows were intended to be a reward for inmates who were on good behavior. It would just be me and a microphone. I told him he should probably look elsewhere. My act, my suburban material, wasn't going to work on prisoners. I didn't think I was the right person for the job. They offered a lot of money, more than I had made on any of my other shows. I asked some of my fellow comedians what to do, and one of them suggested that I tell them to double the money. The thinking was they would say that was too much money and I could get out of it.

But, sure enough, they doubled the money. My jaw dropped, my heart stopped. I was forced into doing the shows. The next day I started to have anxiety attacks. I kept worrying about what jokes I would use. What material would work? The fear of the unknown overtook me. I had never seen the inside of a prison. I had never heard of a comedian working in a prison. I assumed the worst. I had all kinds of thoughts running through my head during the months leading up to the tour. My comedian friends were of no help. It was a big joke to them. They actually fed into my fears, telling me I was going to get shanked. I was scared. I had a dream one night that I got mixed in with the prison population. I was certain that I would not make it back out.

It was an impossible task to write new jokes for this tour because I didn't know what to expect. I didn't know what those guys would laugh at. I was also worried that if I said the wrong thing or made fun of the wrong guy there would be consequences.

Three days and counting before the tour I got a call from my agent, offering me a spot as the opening act for Michael Bolton at the Pittsburgh Civic Arena in front of seventeen thousand people. I jumped at the chance. I'd do anything to take my mind off the prison show. If I'd been offered a job cleaning bathrooms at a strip club, I would have taken it.

The Michael Bolton show was itself a challenge because of the enormity of the room and the stage, not to mention that the audience was coming to hear music, not comedy. I would have to adapt my material to work with this audience. The show went over very well, but I couldn't enjoy the success too much because lurking in the back of my mind was the prison tour.

Thanksgiving came, and I couldn't enjoy the meal or my time with my family because I knew that in two days I'd have to be on stage for an hour in front of murderers and rapists. I began doubting myself. I wasn't sure if I had enough material for a one-hour show. It's a rule of thumb in comedy that you should have at least 30 percent more material than the time allotted for the show. At this point in my career I had no more than an hour's worth of material. Not all of it solid jokes. Still, I hoped that what I had would be enough.

Waking up the morning of the first show, I had an over-whelming sense of doom and fear. I tried to reason with myself. I fought this fear with everything that I could think of. I tried to downplay the show, telling myself that it was "just another show." Okay, so it might be a little more difficult, but I'd been through difficult shows before, I reminded myself. I could handle it. I hoped.

I arrived at the prison just after dark. As requested, I showed up an hour before show time because of all of the security issues. As I approached the gates, I felt like I was being sucked into a black hole. You're not greeted with open arms. At your typical comedy venue, the manager gives you a big handshake and asks how the drive was. Not here. Not a whole lot of smiles. It was all business with these guards. They took my belt, my watch, and a few other things that were metal. And put them all in a box. When I tried to joke with one of the guards, he looked me straight in the eyes and without cracking a smile said, "This is for your protection. One of these animals could take your watch off you and slash you across the face with the band links." At that point I started thinking, "What in God's name am I in for?" The guard then escorted me to the gymnasium. Now I'm thinking, "I hope I don't have to walk past the prisoners and have them whistle and yell at me like in the movies." Thank God we avoided that.

Once I arrived in the gym, we had to wait. Everything in prison is done according to a precise schedule. The guards lined up against the wall, waiting for the prisoners to be led into the gym. I had a guard specifically assigned to me. The prisoners came in and the guards did a head count.

It was a big gymnasium with the bleachers pulled out on one side and a microphone mid court. And that was it. I never felt so alone in a crowd. I looked around the room and I noticed that the guards didn't have any guns. They were carrying billy clubs. I asked one of the guards why he wasn't carrying a gun. He said, "We can't carry guns in here. The prisoners could rush a guard, take his gun, and try to take over the prison. It's been done before."

Just as he said that, I heard the clang of the cell doors opening and then a lot of yelling and screaming. I heard one guy in particular shout, "You better be funny, mother f...er!" My knees started to go weak. I couldn't have run away if I wanted to. I was a prisoner here too.

The prisoners filed in and took their seats. They didn't look particularly happy. If they were happy at all, it was because they had a chance to get out of their cells. Other than that, they didn't look like they were in the mood to be entertained.

There was no introduction for me. I just walked out in front of them and began my act. I opened up by asking them if they watched a lot of TV. Nothing. No response. I plowed through all of my TV material anyway. About three minutes into the show, I started to hear snarls and growls. I kept going, knowing I was using up all of my material way too fast. Under ordinary circumstances, my act would have allowed time for laughter. But there was no laughter. At one point the prisoners began to yell at me, and the thought crossed my mind that they were going to rush the stage. It was a frightening situation. I didn't have the audience on my side and I was not making any of the guards happy either. In fact, the guards were probably a little pissed at me for making their job harder. I started to worry about my safety. I tried my top-of-the-line material. No luck. I went to the blue material, stuff I thought these guys would laugh at. No laughs.

I finished the show after about 35 minutes of hell. The prisoners kind of clapped. A few of the prisoners were kind enough to offer me advice. One guy said, "You better get funny," and another said, " Shit, you ain't goin' nowhere."

I wanted desperately to find a place to hide, but I had to stand there as the prisoners filed past me. It was a humiliating experience. The guy who paid me said, "Wow, I bet that's the easiest money you ever made."

I got my possessions back and returned to my hotel. This is what I wrote in my journal at the end of that day: "The only thing worse that could have happened was if they (the prisoners) had attacked me. I am completely drained. This can't go on. Wow, this is possibly the worst show I've ever done. I was so frightened on stage it kept me from being able to do my job. I am exhausted. They (the comedians) all told me I was crazy for even considering doing this. It looks like they may be right. It's 10:30 and I have to go to bed. I have two shows tomorrow. Hope things go better."

Looking back at that journal entry, I can't believe that was me. I remembered the frame of mind I had been in just three days earlier; I was working in front of seventeen thousand people, feeling like a rock star—limo, flash bulbs, signing autographs. Now I was about as far down the ladder as you can go in the comedy world. Now I was a frightened comedian. I had lost my confidence. Why was I scared? First, I was in uncharted territory. I knew nothing about the crowd. I knew nothing about the room. The prisoners could sense this fear and lack of confidence and they jumped on it. They found my weakness and they attacked me.

If the shows were going to improve, I would have to get my confidence back. But how? My jokes were not cutting it. Even my best stuff was getting groans. I would have to rely on all my years of experience performing on stage. This wasn't going to be easy. I still had to overcome the fear. I don't care how good you are; if you dread taking the stage, you will not win over the crowd.

I was like Grover in *The Monster at the End of this Book*. I had let my anxieties build. I dreaded confronting the monster. And as we know, the monster at the end of the book turned out to be Grover. There was nothing to be afraid of. But I didn't know that at the time. I had let my fear get the best of me and so I was beaten before the show began.

As I was preparing for the next show I started thinking that I should be able to handle this crowd. I started to reaffirm who I was. I thought about how hard I had worked to get to where I was. I called a comedian friend and talked to him about the shows, and he boosted my confidence a bit.

My biggest challenge was figuring out a way to relate to the prisoners. I didn't normally mix with this kind of crowd. I have to figure out what the audience wants.

After a good night's sleep, I woke up with a much better attitude about performing later that day. I felt I could take on the prisoners. It was a daytime show, so already it felt different. I went through the same checkpoints and procedures and then one of the guards told me that the warden wanted to see me before the show. Oh no, this can't be good, I thought to myself. So I went to the warden's office, which looked as sterile and cold as any warden's office you've ever seen in the movies. He offered me a seat and some water. I took the seat but passed on the water. He began by telling me that he had heard about last night's show and how poorly it went. He wanted to cancel the show and the rest of the tour. He called my agent and the two of them went back and forth for a few minutes. I would have been fine if the show was canceled, but my agent didn't want to lose his commission. The show would go on.

While my agent and the warden were battling it out, I thought of a few jokes. I also thought about what a comedian named Barry Berry told me: "You have to make the audience your friend and you have about a minute's worth of time to identify with them. If you don't, you'll spend the rest of the show trying to win them over."

This show was a little different. First of all, I was perform-ing in what can best be described as a game room. It even had a stage. The prisoners were dressed in casual clothes, not prison garb. I opened with a bit about my brushes with the law, thinking this was a way they could connect with me, and these jokes went over okay. I got a few more laughs and then I let them slip away. I worked really hard but the show was so-so. Near the end I looked over at the warden, who gave me the "okay-but-it's-not-really okay" nod. After the show, he shook my hand and said, "So you like doing this kind of work?" I told him it was a challenge and that this was only the second prison show that I have done. By comedic standards it was not a good show. But it was better than the first show.

My confidence started to grow because I could sense what I needed to do. I knew that the more I performed in front of these prisoners, the better the shows would be. I didn't have much time to think about my performance because my next scheduled show was later that day. One thing that concerned me was the crowd's raucousness. During both shows the prisoners talked among themselves and, even worse, yelled crude and rude things at me. I let it all pass without acknowledging the comments. I figured I was better off not needling them and stirring up an already prickly crowd. There were little boundaries here, and they could say whatever they wanted. But so could I. If I didn't say something back to them, I would appear weak. I had to come up with a few zingers, but nothing that would cause a fight or a riot.

That evening's show was another so-so performance. I just battled through it. I wasn't really on my game. A few laughs here and there, but nothing spectacular. My journal entry that day was: "Not a very successful day today. It started out with the warden wanting to cancel the entire tour. The deck looks stacked against me. The prisoners don't really like me. The guards don't really like me. Now the wardens are against me. I'm thrilled to be back in my hotel room. It feels good to see my belongings again."

You can see that Day Two was not much better. I reached out to a few more comedians but they had nothing to offer me. I had to turn this around somehow. I didn't want this to be a black mark on my career. I had seen three audiences, so I sort of knew what to expect. As a result, some of my fear had subsided.

I woke up on Day Three determined to do better. I convinced myself that no one could stop me from having a good show. I didn't care what the guards, the warden, or even the prisoners thought.

The prisoners filed into the room and settled in for my fourth show. The first ten minutes were just like the other shows—a few laughs, but not a rousing success. I did have more energy, though. And then it happened. One of the prisoners, a rather short fellow, said, "We don't want to hear any of this Richie Cunningham shit. We want stuff from the streets." The crowd erupted in laughter. I came back with, "Hey, did Webster say something?" The crowd went crazy. I followed that line with, "Didn't you used to be on *Diff'rent Strokes?*" Even more laughter. I said, "What you talkin' about, Willis? This *is* stuff from the streets." Now I knew what they wanted. They wanted me to top them when they shouted out something. The rest of the show I picked on the little guy. He was having fun with it. I also started tossing out barbs every time one of the prisoners said something. And I wasn't always nice. But that's what those guys understood and that's how they communicated. I spoke their language. To my amazement, instead of these guys wanting to kill me, they were laughing. Every time I came back at them with a zinger the place went bonkers. I had a great show.

Later that day, I wrote in my journal: "A big turnaround has occurred today. Still, not where I want to be, but much, much better. Now that I know what they want, I can communicate with them."

The next show was special. It was in a women's prison. I'd never worked an all-female crowd. I was excited to see what I was in for. As it turned out, this audience was very, very receptive. These gals had a much better disposition than the guys. It was a great show. I was even able to do my material. They were genuinely interested in what I had to say. They didn't yell out anything. It was a good break from the other shows. I wrote in my journal, "This is what I've been looking for. It was like a vacation day today. Lots of smiles. Lots of laughs. Everything's all good." (In all fairness, I have to confess that after the show one of the guards told me not to get too cocky about the enthusiastic response—I was the first man most of these women had seen in a couple of years.)

After a great night's sleep, I was ready to go. I was feeling so good that I thought I'd go out on a limb a little bit and maybe even use a few props. Before the show I had one of the guards lend me his hat and billy club. As the prisoners filed in and the guards were doing their head count, I took the microphone and, in my best Dustin Hoffman *Rain Man* voice, I did a head-count of the prisoners. The prisoners burst out laughing, and the guards chuckled. This was important. The prisoners saw that I was making fun of the guards and this created a bond between me and them for the rest of the show.

The show went on at a regular pace. I did my material in between the banter from the crowd. This was going to be a full-fledged show. Instead of five or ten minutes being funny out of a 45-minute show, almost the whole set was funny. Afterwards a lot of the prisoners came over and shook my hand and thanked me for coming. I was thrilled to be able to entertain these guys and add a little joy to their day.

My journal entry that day recorded this turn-around. "Things are clicking now. I know what I'm doing. I have a few more things to add and let's see if we can end this thing on a high, high note."

The next show I worked the crowd again and used the same props. I even added some music through a song parody. My journal reported, "Excellent show, the best yet. Great raves coming back from my agent and the wardens."

The rest of the shows went equally well. By the end of the tour, I felt as though I had conquered the world. I grew so much as a comedian that week. It was so difficult at the beginning, and then so easy at the end. I know I will never do anything more difficult on stage in my life. Everything that I learned from those shows I shared with you in this book. I hope you can see how you can take a difficult speaking situation and turn it on its head and communicate with your audience more effectively. Knowing what your audience wants and being confident and comfortable with your material will make any speaking engagement a breeze. It's all about the audience. You have to know who they are and give them what they want.

And chances are, you'll never have to face a crowd as tough as this one was. But what you can take from this story is everything I have talked about in this book: practice your material as much as you can, make it entertaining, be prepared for the unexpected, don't be afraid to use props or other visuals, and, above all, know your audience.

MY STORY

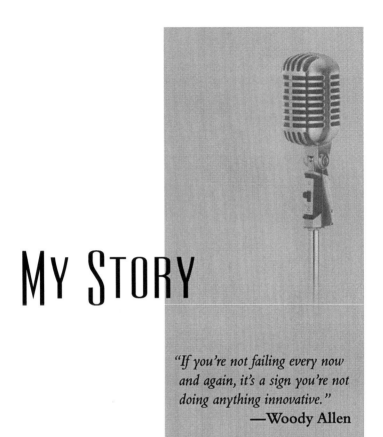

"If you're not failing every now and again, it's a sign you're not doing anything innovative."
—**Woody Allen**

ll I ever wanted to be was a comedian. As a kid I was fascinated by the *Tonight Show*. I can remember my parents sending me to bed and then I would sneak back downstairs to watch the show. I was amazed that guys like Johnny Carson could make you laugh. How did they come up with their jokes? How did they prepare for the show? Where did they perform?

In high school I was never the class clown, but I was funny. I remember writing a few jokes for some friends who were performing in the high school talent show. The enjoyment I got out of hearing my words and making people laugh was incredible. I always knew that I wanted to be a performer. It came naturally to me. The first time I had to stand in front of my classmates and make a presentation in high school I really looked forward to it.

College was no different. My decision to go to the University of Pittsburgh was based on a poster I saw while touring the campus. There was a picture with a microphone and a silhouette of a man playing a guitar advertising a talent show. I thought, "This place is for me." I went to Pitt because I saw an advertisement for their talent show.

I used my time in college to prepare for my stand-up career. I took as many speech and acting classes as I could fit into my schedule. This would have been sheer terror for most of my fellow students. I thought it was exciting. As a matter of fact, one of my professors asked me to help him instruct the class. What I think my fellow students didn't realize is how valuable these speech classes would be. College kids don't understand how important verbal communications skills are to their future success.

One of the reasons that I enjoyed the speech classes so much was the notion I could do it my way. I didn't have to stand behind the podium. I didn't have to do what everyone else was doing. It was up to me to do what I want to do. I may have the same material to deliver but I could present it the way I wanted to. I am the actor, writer, and director. I have total creative control. I thought if I did it a little differently from the rest of the students I could get a response from the crowd. I wanted to get them to laugh. Another reason I enjoyed being in front of the classroom was the rush. I got off on the excitement. I found it exhilarating. It's a test and you have to prove yourself every time you take the stage. For a comedian the reaction is immediate: they either laugh or they don't. There is no better feeling than to hear the roar of applause.

I don't like driving fast in a car. I don't climb mountains. I live for the challenge of being in front of a live crowd. I get juiced from being the guy in the limelight.

With over twenty years of comedic experience behind me I can say that my formal education was incomplete. The professors focused almost exclusively on the performer and the material instead of addressing the audience, which is what the performer should be focusing on. Don't get me wrong. What you say is important but connecting with the audience and making sure they take home your message is more important. You can have the greatest advice in the world but if your audience doesn't take it in, it's not worth anything. If you can't get them to listen why be on stage?

My first time on a real stage was a talent show. My friends were surprised that I tried my hand at stand-up comedy. They marveled at my poise on stage. A few said I looked like a natural on stage. A couple other people said it seemed out of character for me. I remember one guy telling me "You don't do that." I said, "I'm eighteen, I don't do anything yet." Nevertheless I was hooked.

So I was going to classes during the day for my formal education and hitting the comedy clubs at night for my street smarts, if you will. As my talent blossomed I got booked for more and more shows.

Soon after college I began doing comedy full time. As I made my way up the comedy ladder I had the good fortune to work with stars such as Drew Carey, Ray Romano, Jay Leno, Howie Mandel, Dennis Miller, Tim Allen, etc. I was even able to finagle my way into a couple of movies including *Gung Ho, Dominick and Eugene, One for the Money* and *One Shot*. I had my picture in *Cosmopolitan Magazine* with Michael Keaton and George Wendt. I even hosted a morning radio show.

After years of working the comedy circuit I began looking for a little balance in my life. I wanted to settle down. So I entered the business world, where I began sitting through stultifyingly dull presentations and uninspired motivational speeches that motivated me to nod off—but eventually motivated me to write this book, which I hope will help you to become a speaker that will leave people not only laughing, but wanting more.

For more information about David visit:

www.davidmichaellive.com

For booking please contact David or his agent:

davidmichael@live.com

david@talentnetworkinc.com

WA